The Night Surveyor

Christopher North

For Virginia & Jan
Well met at Alnucua
Vella

Alvazor

September 2016

Oversteps Books

First published in 2014 by   Oversteps Books Ltd
6 Halwell House
South Pool
Nr Kingsbridge
Devon
TQ7 2RX
UK

www.overstepsbooks.com

Printed in Great Britain by imprint digital, Devon

For Marisa
and in memory of my father and mother,
Arthur and Pat North

Acknowledgements:

Axes won first prize in the 1996 Northwards poetry competition judged by Ian Crichton Smith. *Scrub Clearance* won first prize in the initial New Forest Poetry Society Open Poetry Competition in 1996. *Collecting the Forest* won first prize in the first Kickstart poetry competition judged by Matthew Sweeney in 1998. *February 10th 1963* won first prize in the Ways With Words short story competition judged by Julia Stoneham in 2005. *The Photographer* won first prize in The Mayor's Prize Enfield judged by Mario Petrucci in 2011. *Encounters with Venerable Trees* won second prize in the Yorkshire poetry competition judged by Michael Symmons Roberts in 2011. *Berners' Doves* won the short poem prize in the Flamingo poetry competition judged by Peter Daniels and Mimi Khalvati in 2013. *Census* was second prize winner in The Poetry on the Lake festival competition judged by Anne-Marie Fyfe in 2013. Poems in this collection also appeared in *Tears in the Fence, Smith Knoll* and *Poetry Nottingham* now *Assent Poetry Magazine*.

Contents

1

Birthday Party Photograph 1955

Fronting pink floral wallpaper,
sitting on a gold threaded three seater,
standing behind, sitting in front —
we were singing.

The girl with a lazy eye and spread fan,
the girl who married a famous film director,
the boy from opposite whose mother was nervy,
the boy who played the banjo:
in our school uniforms,
we were singing.

The girl with a Minnie Mouse ribbon,
the boy my parents liked
who was from a different school
and had a better bike (Sturmey-Archer gears)
who I didn't like —
we were all singing.

And I cannot hear a word of it,
not even a faint echo.

Parents looked down:
the girl who went to Canada,
the boy who had an operation to flatten his ears —

in front of mock Regency curtains,
in front of the twin bench recliner,

we were singing.

Axes

My brother and I pushed drawing pins
into the upright's hammer felts —
it was what you did to make it sound
like Winifred Atwell but we couldn't
play it. We just stumbled through the
boogie-woogie low notes.

In the thirties, grandfather's Willesden
fishmongers specialized in dressed crabs
and fresh mackerel from Billingsgate.
Beneath his Homburg he chopped metallic heads,
cleaver in his massive hand
and whistling round his cigarette.

And whistling too, the boiling crabs as
upstairs piles of 'Fish Trader's Gazette'
grew in the throne room, raised bowl
with nouveau swirls and royal crest, beside
an ash-tray and his spectacle case.
His hands were dry, pale and scaly,

smelling of fish gore but able,
when spread to cover a keyboard octave.
He played 'The Lost Chord' or
'Bird in a Gilded Cage'
down at the Coach and Horses
among stouts and bowls of winkles.

Thirty years later my brother and I
were idly twanging the upright's wires
making horror movie sound effects when
the stair outside creaked.
What you two up to? wheezed my grandfather
from the threshold, wafting in stale smoke
and the faint odour of fish paste.

Do you know 'Piano-Tuner's Boogie' grandad?
Homburg tipped back, he hit the drawing-pinned keys.
His curl of Woodbine fell:
God's truth, what you done to this?
Cancer got him two years later and two years

after that we passed the upright through
a toilet seat; a rag-day stunt. It was what
you did then, my brother and I,
in a shoal of students, wielding axes.

Stardust

When Catherine was small
she liked silver stars;

she had a box of silver stars.
She would put them inside

her endless gifts to classmates
or sprinkle them on a dob of glue,

tongue one side of her mouth
as she wrapped and bowed each new

present on our dining table.
And errant stars would fall

down to the desert wastes of floor.
And they became one with all

the dust and musty flotsam,
the casual shifting fluff and drift,

caught in corners with dross and slough.
So years later in the skirting crack

we found a hardened rubber band,
a Spanish coin, a rusted tack

and the glinting silver stars.
And the perfect silver stars,

though dust from dust, gave specks of light
as an autumn evening moved to night.

On Seeing Ben Hartley's 'Woman at a Pump'

i.m. of my mother Pat North, 1923 - 2000

We've painted our new house blue.
Blue is now our daily colour
as I think it has been always.
Children always paint water blue
and this woman, who must be a mother,
is in a blue world
pumping wind-caught water.

That childhood cottage
with the pump by the door
that headed the path to the lane,
the lane that ran to the river
that we painted blue
in the picture of 'our house'
together with obvious large flowers.

And as she pumps,
as she pumped,
the woman who was mother
didn't sense the wind that tugged her apron
and sprayed the water into a doorstep soak
nor notice our cat coming up from the river
with an opalescent trout.

Now it's blue, blue that we love,
blue behind our blue-black railings.
My mother pumped the morning pump,
drove a blue love through everything —
a blue that drives through it all,
a seamless almost shadow-less blue
beside a bucket on a soaked step.

Towards Clarity

It rains.
Or is it in fact rain?
Is each drop less than half a millimetre in width?
Are there more than 1000 drops per cubic yard?
So is it drizzle? And has it stopped or is it now rain
gradually becoming drizzle? When exactly
does it stop? When precisely does it start
and become rain?

I am here:
Ref. 982081 on sheet 165
although that assumes this plan is correct.
Anyway it can't be more accurate than
say fifteen metres either way —
to scale, the size of a pencil point
and it doesn't allow for curves.
Everything is curved.

It's 5.10:
as I've been thinking this, it's already become later
and anyway that's by my watch which, like
every functioning watch, is very rarely correct.
If it is, I cannot be certain it is because
in checking against others I must consider
the overwhelming majority of watches
that are wrong.

So do you love me?
Tell me truly.

Truth Game

Come on, you never tongue-kissed your mother!
The sea beyond the streaked glass, steel beneath black.

Laughter broke the smoky air at our every beginning —
our late night dialogue a convoy under bombardment

by invisible American students in the lounge,
we in the snug with our overwhelming question.

I snorted coke once but it made me throw up
and then a silence with just one nervous giggle.

We locked eyes until the next blurted confession.
I once balled my best friend's date and didn't tell her.

How good was it? C'mon, c'mon! A seethe of voices,
a wave receded and stones glistened raw as offal.

Just Before Jane Left for Shanghai

Hadn't seen her for six years.

I thought of her as essence of Sidcup
(quiet beep of a passing car, a twitter of sparrows)
but now she leaves for Shanghai in three days
to assist in the growing Sino craze for horse racing.
Didn't you know that I love riding — the turf, all that?
For them it's early days — they have a sort of tote
but it's rudimentary. Superb stables though —
just need management.
She shows me her quick reference guide to Mandarin.
Just for three months anyway, then Beijing to see the sights,
and on to Hong Kong, Singapore, Sydney —
all the usual airports — I'll be in California by May.

Then I was talking to David just back from Barcelona
where finally he'd cleared up that complicated fraud case.
He recounted the story of a man, very club tie and credible,
notorious alumnus of his son's private school in Scotland,
who ended a chequered career forging ancient
Chinese manuscripts in a tiny flat in what was then Peking,
for collectors in the West. Fooled them for years.
Very 'Hitler's Diaries' David concluded,
but he'd eked out a life. It's not known what he was escaping from.

Only eight hours later I picked up the Australian poet
who arrived at Heathrow before dawn — *to Singapore great,*
but after that it was cattle class — who'd just watched
an in-flight film about Elizabeth the First. He needed
to download its imagery in the car back to Chalfont.
I think they got her about right — and then over coffee
we discussed geese (this house was a goose farm once).
In a way I was raised by geese he murmured finally
before going off for a long sleep in the back room
with its view of cherry trees and February primroses.

I can see her on a gallop — her lop-sided smile,
but I can't make out the buildings behind.
I can see her arrival in Los Angeles,
she'll be well travelled by then — it won't surprise.
I can see her outside, hailing a cab, the cabby
laughing as he loads the boot — then they drive away,
me seeing it as clearly as the desk in the other room
where I need to work on a budget. I know once I start
I will have its very edge and flavour by the end of the day.

Berners' Doves

When dawn pinches the top branches
between thumb and forefinger,

the Balsam shivers just for a moment
before trees' night shadows liquefy

as light enters their cage —
it's then I would like his turquoise doves,

rose pink doves and lime green doves
to burst from the hawthorn thicket,

cross the dim lawns to the Field Maple
I planted ten years ago

to roost there, murmuring to one another
long enough for me to count them.

A Walk Near Chequers

Here the scarp doesn't want anxiety.
The clear and levelled paths, dozy trees
and Chequers, squat and content,
seem bedded in orderliness —
a Chiltern vale with cottages, kissing gates
and trim farms.
Scabious, cranes-bill, hawks-bit
point the wash of landscape with their
watercolour specks as if it hung
in a county tea shop.

       And so a fine October day
       becomes banal, wanting more, it has a taint,
       a yawn of discontent.

       Maybe a glimpsed
alignment would enliven: tumuli, steeple,
a farm gate and through a lynchet meadow
a line drawn to a snow streaked summit.

       No. It needs explosion:
pluming flames from the mansion window,
or groaning lovers deep in the buckthorns;
hedges writhing into forest,
the thin whine of distant wolves

and buzzards circling, lower and lower,
the yearling's paddock.

Moving Father to Sunrise

He'd been hanging all hope on this Friday, not knowing
it would be a day of road accidents — ambulances bleating,
stunned drivers sitting on verges among
urgent men with clipboards and fluorescent jackets.

We'd tramped vanishing point corridors
from North Building to South Building
of the Queen Alexandra asprawl at the foot of a cliff
topped with Victorian bastions and gun emplacements.

Two more anonymous passages found his frail figure
on a bed. Then, bewildered by sudden open air, he'd taken an age
to ease himself into the car, fumbling to fasten his belt.

From Cosham we passed the grassed over Palmerston Forts
and yet another collision near the Museum of Explosions.

We waited in the Sunrise reception as a lady with a jigsaw
told us her husband watched news on the hour
every hour but remained quite serene and unaware
of credit crunches, MP's shenanigans or other disasters.
He sleeps in 'Reminiscence', is locked in at night.

So to the room, television squat in the corner,
welcoming orchid, busy nurses that removed his clothes
as *it's been a long day and he needs a rest.*
Leaving, we passed a bored pianist at a baby grand
and inmates weakly singing *I Have Often Walked* ...

To end this day of delivering our loved senescent
from hospital purgatory to hopeful, more tranquil pastures,
we ate at *Thank God Its Friday*. They had a Jack Daniels special.
Do you sauce the chicken with bourbon? I asked.

Bending low for our order, like a primary teacher
attending children with their colouring books
and ready to mop any mess they'd made, she let go a trained
little laugh and in a practised, grown up voice said:
Oh I don't think so, I don't think so.

88th Birthday in Sunrise

In this place of silent forms in chairs
          every shade is dulled and mute.

Those strange familiars seem concerned
          but soon become swinging doors.

That tree the window frames,
          just out of reach —
                you know that once you knew its name.

A Death

It is the silence of the dead that gives them this air;
their triumphant silence, proof against any questioner
in the world.

Keith Douglas 1920 - 1944

A mortar fragment felled him in a second
beside a hedge near St Pierre, south of Bayeux
and thus he missed:

the returning odour of a south-east breeze,
the torpor and fog of his first year back
finding indifference, a dull ordinariness

but then a face with understanding eyes,
a south country church door, a waiting car
and so year would have followed year —

each a tumbled box of door-keys, buff files,
formal letters, letters waited for, voices,
some dinners in memorable places,

apple blossom, its quick confetti
noticed a certain day each spring, her laugh,
a weekend with two friends, one funny, one quiet,

a pub in Dovedale with a sullen landlord,
their stay that became an annual ritual,
a photograph he realised would adorn his fly-leaves,

a gilded hall in an antique park with clumped elms,
blue midland landscapes then a garden wall,
his child's first shaky bicycle ride

and the way the books grew, rank on rank,
beside the fire-irons, the portrait,
and talk about new voices — Hughes, Larkin,

Eleanor Rigby. Then a friend's Gloucester funeral,
meeting comrades from Zem Zem
— seeing them differently, a daughter's wedding,

a brief assignation, a letter from Bishop,
visits to India, Kyoto, a farm in Bunyah,
a round at St Andrew's, fishing the Taw,

surprising applause from a packed Sheldonian,
a seamless week in Aix-en-Provence,
the full 'Collected', a reading with Heaney,

fountain pen, paper knife, the London Library,
the Sherwood's reunion, a first computer,
        a vase he knew somehow would outlive him.

Scrub Clearance

For elders use cutters and pick;
slice whippy new shoots and drag away
then lever out the trunk from base.
The ones close up to the haws are worst
as the roots mesh under and the crown
tangles in the brush where it can't be reached.
These are best tackled section by section.
The top comes down easier if left a month to dry.
Pull out seedlings with your hands;
be thorough as elders grow quickly.

With brambles, hook back tendrils
to find node points. With the pick lift them
then pull steadily to take out secondary roots intact.
One node feeds a system ten yards across
so once removed, ground seems liberated.
Dog-rose briars have to be tugged down.
This must be gentle as the briars easily snap.
They come in a mass of rambler and hips;
more than you believe could be up there
and clear sky suddenly breaks in.

Having gained space, dead wood can be removed.
Some oaks have stagged tops hanging aslant;
you need to hack with a bill-hook at the break
and when they fall, clean the cut.
Other over-canopied oaks will be dead
and can be pushed over after rocking.
They often break in half on landing
and are surprisingly easy to carry away.
When they are gone the wood-scape changes;
you can see further, sound trees can be counted.

Stack brush and old timber for burning.
In a clear space make a furnace of dryer sticks
then add gradually the elder, rose and bramble
along with logs of decayed timber.
At the end of the day you can stack the mound
with leaf mould so it smoulders slowly;
the fine ash it makes will be good fertilizer.
It's important to clear as you work;
as you do fields, the houses across the valley
and the hills beyond become visible,

suddenly explicable and in order.

Index: Beechwood

2

Collecting the Forest

On my tower thrust deep in the white-beam canopy
I place my easel where there's filtering to the light
then flood the canvas glaucous green mixed with white
like the green of young corn or stained verdigris.

I work in clouds of deeper green washed over pale,
then, with finer point, etch the prayer hands
of swelling leaves over the grey-green bands
of colour then the umbel's veined and silver grail.

Where, with eased explosion, flowers have opened,
I catch each stamen with tungsten line of ink,
each calyx, anther and filament then link
with careful crosshatch the subtle shadow-blend.

In my airy place these things are accomplished
until their light merges with the light around
and when it's clear the tree's essence has been found
and marked to every detail, I declare it finished

and I burn it. Then fell the tree.

I turn to the limbs of oak, their new budding
on a fuzz of twigs, uncurling wet and ragged
leaves, letting surrounding green be dragged
from profound spring light that is round them flooding.

They fleck the muscularity of squat boughs
and, after catching this with fine and hair line brush,
every atom of its structure intricate on light that's lush;
canvas melts, oak crashes to a carpet of woodland flowers.

I etch cherry dark beneath boiling inflorescence,
seeking to trap all the blossom's quivers,
my brush working and reworking the shiver
of twig tips and falling petals in twilight scents.

I grasp as I can the flicker of days and quarters
locked so tight in cells and ramifying veins;
the split of seed an unfolding bud explains,
leaves turning through their chemistry and waters.

I capture, burn and fell; turn to maple, birch and beech;
fell and burn them too, yearning for every tree in reach.

I cram the ashes into my box of elm,
ashes crammed like a million layers of leaf,
packed tight to bursting to secure this belief
that I own the ash and the ash's realm.

To capture every tree! Every species of tree!

Books Fall and Crack

A book must be the axe for the frozen sea within us.
                                                    Franz Kafka

Yes, admit books,
sculptures of books, some monumental, seen above trees,
considered as landmarks, glimpsed through a cleft in hills.

Or books as a row of terraced dwellings
founded on mud, yellow clay or deep cretaceous;
books in a flock, a welter, an electric storm
crackling over rock pinnacles.

Books as high flying objects caught in a turning thermal
or seen as the weave and rush of a murmuration, as dust-motes,
dust in the air, an approaching sandstorm,
a tornado of books howling across the Great Plain,
sucking up roofs, trucks, people.

Find book stacks, crags, screes of pages, leaves of book thickets
skirting down-slopes in colophon, prefaces, footnotes;
a book avalanche at dawn in a valley no-one lives in
so no one sees the thunderous tumbling.

Watch books swarm across the orchard, seething, writhing,
crawling across each other, books as air surrounding everything,
books as asteroids on crazed orbits — some desolate, cratered,
some iron clad, others vaporizing or burning up.

And on down-lands beyond a smudge of city,
book towers in word meadows,
clouds drifting over their tranquil rectos, versos
and the calligraphy of ancient meadows, inscribed sheepfolds,
scribbled villages and bustling unconcerned High Streets.

Sarah Closely Observed

Wriggles her shoulders – squinches up,
        then releases them.

She's flamboyant with her cigarette,
        experiments with mouth shapes,

then settles for a thirty second frown of concentration.
        She murmurs dreamily after fifteen.

There's a minor re-slump then with tiny sideways shakes,
        an affirmative tongue-and-roof *tut tut*.

The background remains solidly noisy and chair scraping.
        She adjusts to quizzical,

indeed becomes invaded with quizzicality. It ends
        with a big, wide macaque laugh,

head back and teeth that suddenly
        fill the table's universe

and it's teeth and more teeth until, abruptly,
        she tucks them away.

Group silence arrives like curtains being drawn
        and the company emits mild, empathetic sighs.

She extinguishes the cigarette
        as if mildly tapping a gavel

and then moves fast. Leaning forward and looking across the
        table's wide and littered landscape:

Changing the subject completely ...
        she begins.

After Discussing Painting
For Patricia Sentinella

From my window,
suddenly,
a white pheasant
amongst snowdrops.

Mid-ground
my eye sweeps
a frosted roof
and on my sill
these words inked
on a lined page.

I would like
a bowl of oranges
to place beside
the white pheasant.

Evening Conversation, Great Lawn, Dartington

At the vague point when the light drained away,
trees became silhouettes of themselves
and surrounding conversation disembodied.
She dropped a register, became earnest:
Listen, there isn't an idea in what I'm saying,
I don't want you looking for an idea.

I pictured a bookless place with flies,
collapsed blinds and chevron linoleum
but rejected them as not her voice — she's Sussex Weald,
hunter trials, a ha-ha, lavender knot, rustic tiles.
Like suddenly the power's off, clouds stop,
a paragraph I think I'm into dries up mid-word ...

Was this a barren river flowing with dust and stones
or a locked room in a wisteria swagged dovecote?
... I mean the hills surrounding, the delphiniums,
the cars in the garage, the Pinot Noir,
those fat little cartons from Amazon,
I mean, I look around at this day to day stuff

and it's all so fucking meaningless.
But those bluebell woods! That downland ridge —
the four by four will get you to Midhurst library,
there's Radio Three, there's your morning pages.
Words! I do words — all evening on 'futile',
its etymology — you know, all its possible associations.

The Night Surveyor: Dartington Gardens
For Ben Okri

After the farewell party we grabbed a bottle
and, on your suggestion, headed into the gardens,
pitch dark, rustling leaves — I don't know how many came.

Giggling, without a torch, we found the Tiltyard,
above us Cassiopeia, a slumped Great Bear.
Now be our night surveyor you said.

I declared to the six (or were there seven?):
*'The Cypress is twenty metres from the twelfth Apostle;
the fountain, two chains, fifteen eleven.*

Starlit dunes of Devon fields gleamed above trees
as we crossed silvered lawns and I announced:
we are four hundred feet above the sea

then led them up endless steps, finding risers with gentle kicks.
There's this place of seven echoes someone whispered.
Someone counter-whispered: *No there's six.*

Full fathom five! I shouted from the bastion.
No please not that one surveyor, you murmured.
O trees of dark coral made? — No try something else.

Some bow or brooch or braid or brace, lace, latch or catch...
No echo but a leaden voice climbed inside my ear.
Over Staverton or Berry Pomeroy's lowly thatch

hung Jupiter. No Venus, or was it Mars?
One shouted: *I embrace the universal me,*
voice cracked and small beneath the dome of stars.

Two melted into trees — we remaining passed round wine.
The town below lolled in sodium as if bathing
and you yawned: *Get us back surveyor, I think it's time.*

I counted steps. Shadows rose and fell in bands.
Feeling for damp and stone, plotting silhouettes
in darkness, gradually we became a chain of hands.

Census

Other items sent in by people included credit cards, cheques, a set of deeds, family photographs, a completed driving licence application form ....

Office of National Statistics April 2011

... and some sent small cellophane packets of toenail clippings.
There were locks of hair, a train ticket from Paddington,
a shirt button (white) and a small plastic tub
of collar studs and cuff-links.

There were copies of expired contracts, X-rays of persons
now deceased, a group photograph of a wedding
— only the photographer's company identified,
a concern long since out of business.

And restaurant bills, small pieces of fabric
from an heirloom counterpane, a condom wrapper
and an empty box of 'Three Castles' cigarettes,
the gold foil still intact.

Then the poems, and diaries, and bundles of letters
— even four hundred typed pages of a novel that began:
At four o' clock it rained. It was always raining.
She wanted it to stop but it continued relentlessly ...

There were children's Xmas cards with glued tinsel
and a box of journals filled with minute,
inked handwriting in German.

Some delivered personally bore effulgent floral tributes,
in one case accompanied by a small man
in a Charlie Chaplin costume who performed a little dance,
clicked his heels and asked the desk clerk to sign
an attendance sheet fixed to a clipboard.

There were offers of liaisons in dim hotels near King's Cross,
a week in Gomera, an invitation to a Hopi ear candle session
and on one occasion the conveyance of an entire midlands
country estate including three miles of trout stream.

Some bestowed hope, atonement, apology – prayers
to a wide range of deities and promises of pilgrimage
to Guadalupe, Santiago, Jerusalem

and there were offers of world peace, universal Karma,
the melodic spread of a benign and loving cosmos
– a caring eternity.

Central Park: Red Bird

July, late July
and heat in the air
beneath such eloquent boughs —

We'd just been hearing fusion raga,
not from the open seats
but as we passed in the shade.
She was for returning,
I was dragging my feet.

Things happen randomly
but if you look hard enough
there's always a pattern
that fits like a plugged-in plug.

Of course one is aware of hustling possibilities;
they're part of a city's continuum.
They come dressed corporate, in beachwear,
as derelict or glam and tired eyed;

that little thicket of words: hustle, bustle, hassle, tussle
all somehow in the mix. There's always the memory
of having been hooked before,
knowing you've been caught, been the mug.

He was slim, contingent, with a bright red perfect tie
and a pink band to his Panama;
his shirt eye-wincing white against a cream jacket
striped with soft blue stripes and perhaps a size too small.
His shoes gleamed, reflecting those eloquent boughs.

There is often distant music.
There are always poems.

Well hi you two! My you're good-looking folks,
why, can I ask you a favour?

It really won't take a minute
and hell it's not costing you anything.
I would like your opinion on something.
Now tell me what you think of this poem I have.

I thought why not,
she voiced a doubt.
Those gracious trees, a park bench:
'In memory of Arnold Klopstock,
my life-mate, my best friend'

And there we sat, two unsettled birds.
Why this piece, you know
I could have written this specifically for you – specifically,
so why don't I just dedicate it to you here and now.

He read like a hammy Hamlet always mid-soliloquy
but with a corner of his eye on us.
It was about a moonlit, travel poster beach and palms
and walking hand in hand through creamy waves,
sand between our toes etcetera and so on,
ending sitting back to back, and as he added,
heart to heart — it was the best line.

Now did you like that?
It was for you;
I felt in my deepest soul that it was for you.

Something has to measure
beneath the heat, beneath the trees.
Dollars changed hands.
I gave him a photograph of our house.

O my O my O my he said.
shaking his head in faux disbelief.

Eloquence of trees — their gracility,
the sun's warmth beneath them
and on one close branch a bright red bird,
contemplating the endless traffic.

The Woman from Phoenix

And it's true, in '85 the agency sent me to Russia
where I fell on the steps of a monument at Tomsk State.
So stupid. I'd been explaining our policy
on raising female awareness in collegiate scenarios
when I tripped, dammit, near that statue
of Lenin with his hand reaching out.
Anyways next thing I found myself on a gurney
naked and encircled by twelve white coats.

You will please now turn over.

Brisk hands felt and probed
my shoulder blades, my neck
and then each vertebra in sequence —
top to bottom, each one, one by one
tweaked, prodded and pinched.
Comment was made in low awed voices.

They say you have the finest back in Siberia.

And it's true their murmuring seemed like admiration
as the kneading continued, each bone, bone by bone.

*Our women work very hard unlike you American women,
our women cannot therefore enjoy a back such as yours.*

I explained about my work-outs, my yoga,
my dietary time-tables.

*In America the workers are exploited,
they do not have backs such as yours.*

I thought of fat women back in Phoenix;
I was wincing with pain but had to laugh.

Released I waited in out-patients for a cab.
A smiling woman came towards me.

She reached forward and lifting my arms,
pulled up my sweater. I let her do it, why not?
Her friends crowded round
as her nails drew lines up and down
my spine. There were intakes of breath.

Our women
are not as well nourished as women in America.

It's true there was some laughter, friendly I think,
and, after smiles, they eventually moved away.
One shouted something, they then laughed loudly.

My lover licks the base of my back,
the lumbar area just above the crease.
I love your back he says.

I have the most beautiful back in Siberia.

Translation from a Papyrus
Found in Memphis, the city of Ptah, believed New Kingdom 1100 BC

... *(hear you passing?)* from the place I have
by your father's walls

It is as the cranes fly —
                    their steady beat of wings

It is like the spring waters —
                    in our abundant pastures

It is like the breeze —
                    in the rushes yonder

and I hear you passing

                    *

I have scented the altar stones
beside your father's walls

It is the scent of honey —
                    from my full honeycombs

It is the scent of sandalwood —
                    just after soaking

It is the scent of the young river —
                    when lilies line its banks

I have poured my scents on the altar
before your father's walls

                    *

Have you seen me
in the shadow of your father's walls

I have waited —
                through the high arch of summer
I have waited —
                through the pinks of dawn and dusk
I have waited —
                for the smallest sign or word

You have not seen me
(in the shadow of your father's walls?)

Photographer

The left kerb frames.
    Catch the trees though
and the lamp post with the blast hole.

Put the boy left, just off foreground —
    has to be seen first,
the kerb directs — his face, that thigh.

Then to the cart,
    the bent up bicycle wheel,
the other, spokes splayed out.

Need those houses. Essential horizon.
    Mount the lens higher,
need more depth of field.

F22 — 1/30th sec — 40mm

The one with the hipped roof first.
    Could be Hemel Hempstead,
must have that.

The eye goes along the other houses,
    sees the garden trees, then tracks back,
sees the tank.

Now the soldier, his helmet,
    the gun turret.
He's looking right at you.

Then what will the eye do?
    Go back to the boy?
No, it's caught by the other body.

It's by the jeep
    with the treaded spare tyre.
Can't see it's face.

So you're back to the cart,
    the boy, the bare thigh —
could be asleep,

then maybe the fallen leaves,
    some muddied like just after rain.
I have my shot.

Could crop out the stretcher.

Encounters with Venerable Trees

This is a fruit knife madam, it wouldn't cut a cabbage"

George III to an unsuccessful assassin.

As we conversed
it became abundantly clear
that my Lord Carob
had a remarkable
breadth of knowledge.

It is true that his utterances
remained firmly
within a Latin based lexicon
and that, in consequence
the arguments proffered

occasionally became
convoluted and centrifugal —
but we remained impressed
by the subtle warp and weft
of his judgements.

He circumnavigated,
made discreet cannonade
and saturated the basic pleadings
with his sweet and podded arguments.
Appeal seemed irrelevant.

The oleander recorder
sat patiently jigging
and jittering
thus everything was captured.
'I am a creature of pods ...'

(as he murmured we nodded sagely)
' ... and have graced this inland sea
since the days of ice.
To stand in judgement Sir,
is both a privilege and duty.'

That multitude sucking and sipping mud,
lining the river — sip sip sip — what!
A hoi polloi, that grim, unsavoury mob.

We found them an awkward orchestra —
woodwind petulant,
timpani impertinent,
a discordance in the brass
and second violins
a rank of nodding fools.

Baton raised we made to guide
this assembly into the divine.
There was a shifting stillness.
We waved the looping baton higher,
gave them all the passion
we could reasonably muster.

The result Sir: a sylvan cacophony.
Music is the godliest art —
dwells in heaven, not the gloomy
purgatories of that 'Swan of Avon'
but our company were clods,
We should send them packing.

The carriage that day —
Spring we do aver,
they were dancing as we passed
those maidens in the meadows —
spinning, the noble earth
spinning around them.

Your majesty seems a little pale;
Perhaps the journey to Windsor —
the roads and dust,

pray rest awhile, We'll send for
James, to bring counterpane
and perhaps some hock and biscuits.

Let us talk for we like to talk,
have talked for days on end —
amongst the trees, what!
Say nothing – they say nothing,
we talk into nothing,
so let us converse awhile
as men do.

Alight here my dear old comrade.
We will sit upon the grass. What!
You wish to stand?
Do you think that wise?
You wish to stand? Stand is that?

A grey breeze moves through
the columned precincts, the gracious courts
of this proud and whispering grove

Bob

is obsessed with weighing things,
his notebook neatly filled
with the weight of toothbrushes,
nail files, tweezers, each potato
of his midday lunch
and, on one epic occasion, his car.

He weighs himself, of course,
using three set scales laid side by side,
each a different make
purchased from three separate suppliers
in three different towns.
He averages results, makes a graph
of morning and evening records.

He seeks the essence of things.
The most basic quality of anything is weight
he declares, *it's what glues us here.*

He weighed a feather found in his front yard
by weighing his shoe, placing the feather inside
then weighing it again, then taking a mean
from five separate sessions all scheduled under
'Miscellaneous found items.'
He weighs individual cigarettes, different brands.
It's interesting, he says,
you'd be surprised at the differences.

The world turns, the oceans don't fly off,
everything coming out the volcano falls back eventually.

Naturally he checks all stated weights on packaging —
they call me Mr Sunshine at the grocer's,
then chuckles to himself as he prepares to weigh
his just-that-morning laundered underpants.

The Portrait

Because the day was overcast
she consented to a session in the Orangery.

At the maid's calling she ran across the rose garden
and through the doors.

The dress, on a mannequin, stood in the corner;
she hated the grubby lace, the dirty pearls.

Here said his gentle voice
and pointing to a chair, *now stand here just so.*

He placed a wooden spoon in her right hand
and moved her arms into place.

The room was still. She could hear shouts from the orchard:
James and the dogs — the carriage was away again

so James was free. The artist's eye flicked up and down.
A peacock butterfly alighted on his palette.

She giggled and he frowned
but then with deft strokes caught that moment

her laugh was fading but not quite faded.
Enough for today he grunted taking the spoon.

His student finished the dull brocade, the grey ruffs;
added a standard posy of flat impossible flowers.

Orchid

'Soldier's satyrion' – Orchis militaris, was known to have grown in Harefield, Middlesex but disappeared in the 19ᵗʰ century.

Beneath tall oaks lining my Lord Egerton's estate
The Royal Progress inched along a field margin,
Their voices travelling over the greening corn.

Amidst a flutter of courtly laughter,
My Lady Margaret's daughter gathered a satyrion
For her Queen.

A sudden grin revealed sugar-blackened teeth
And ringed fingers touched one speckled homunculus:
Adieu my little courtier and she plucked it off.
Then one by one, all the others,
Casting the blossoms onto roadside clay.

Icknield Encounter

I walked Icknield Way deep in summer,
the middle of the day, downland tranced,
the long scarp that ends the bowl of London
running north in drowsed seas of barley.
This was the green way under Wainhill,
I thinking of browsing cattle, cow parsley,
the blurred smudge of horizon glanced.

A figure approached on the ancient way,
centering a silence, walking toward me
with steady rhythm through summer motes.
Drawing nearer I noted clothes of curious cut,
loosened tie, jacket, buttoned waistcoat,
his face tanned and angular, hair receded,
eyes lost as if fogbound in steeps and shires.

He glanced. Our eyes met for a moment.
He made a ghost of smile as if to speak
but willow-herb, betony, meadowsweet
seemed to crowd the space between us
and seeds and spikes of pink and cream,
the fleshy trunk of a massive beech
and loud drone of meadow bees.

The wisp of smile faded to blankness
as he entered a dreaming country
of misty counties and cathedral trees.
Catching the bob of a Chalk-hill blue,
I watched it spread freckled wings
and turning to make banal remark,
became ice cold as winter wind in sedge.

I met just empty furrows, hardened ruts,
the ribbon of Icknield, a distant hanger
but no figure in suit of curious cut,
no buttoned waistcoat nor sun-burned face,
the place contained a vacancy — I was alone.
Later passing a gabled barn, finger written
on a dusty pane: *Yes, I remember ...*

and, of course, a blackbird sang.

Laugharne Stopover

Supper at Brown's —
the juke box thumped
and at the bar, belly over belt,

shirt-tail flagging
the sullen girls, he sang a sweaty
Mama I killed a man ...

He had a good pub voice.
Outside tall youths
creaked in their leathers.

That afternoon no hawk on fire,
no priested shoreline — just a gate
on the crest opening to sky.

I'd seen the word-spattered hut
but the boat-house was closed
so I booked a room below St John's Hill

then turned in early
to read some Wallace Stevens
in a polished, dust-free room.

In the morning drove away west
passing barbed wire Pendine —
the caravans of Amroth.

We Accompany the Visiting American Poet to the Plaza Bar

Jeez, Can't anybody take a joke anymore?

John Ashbery 'Dinosaur Country'

Rounding the corner he flinches as a reflex
but this proves an over-reaction. Actually the graffiti is muted,
not angry — colours selected sepia, various pinks
embellished with beguiling rococo flourishes.

Four dumb people sit on the kerb displaying
their very own species of hopeless inanity. They were like
a small pile of scrubbed, peeled but totally unwanted potatoes.
Background radiation olive-based and domestic,

as dust molecules move in a busy cloud above some wilting things.
Anxiety streams from the paisley cravat as we pass trinket trays
and our progress to the plaza assumes an expected filmic quality.
As always most of the real action is off-lens:

all hidden tinkering with sprockets, knuckled chair leg lathes,
busy entablatures and cornices. Above a swiftless sky
then just one yellow-black squawking creature that hurtles
like something clumsily thrown into the oleander.

So we arrive and play out our arrival endlessly.
This is mostly table shifting, indeed we make a dance
out of table shifting as if manipulated by a system of levers
for after all we are at core city folks — wired up and calibrated.

These moments climax with slices of French omelette.
Once seated we become cardboard. Towards our folds, edges
and outliers come creeping entities that spray-can gaudy runes
over our elevations, façades and exploded cross sections.

Wind murmurs as if through an army of raised forks,
we become numb with granting small permissions.
Bring forth our poisons Charlie! and we creak to starboard.
The moon squats. Someone hums tunelessly in the brambles

then there's a fierce scuffle involving stabs and claws —
that clumsy bird! All agree it has malice written all over it.

3

February 10th 1963

I could have done it.

From sitting there looking out the window at the voiceless snow – the white dunes of it making the garden silent and the drifting thick even beneath the hornbeams; I could have got up from the chair where I was slumped in boredom.

As the sky outside began to darken and pencil lead greyness descended, I could have stood up, my feet on the waxed herring-bone wood-blocks, walked past the new walnut veneer hi-fi stereogram with 'New World Symphony' fresh from its sleeve (view of Yosemite Park), gone into the kitchen, slid a pound note from my mother's purse, found the A to Z on the kitchen shelf, slunk upstairs, put on that dark green pullover with black piping, found the sixth form school scarf, donned the shortie raincoat, pulled the gum boots out of the utility room with its loose door-handle and then, without a word, wrapped myself up and creaked off down the drive leaving the family slumped in their post roast beef slumber.

I could have passed between the chain-link fences, dividing off the numbed gardens of 31 and 37 and at the end turned right down the hill passing the winter trees in the wooded plot on the corner and trudged to the end of the road beneath the water-colour greyness of low cloud. I could have walked on the road because the pavements were icy and the clearest track was where the cars had gone. I could have passed the golf course on the right, a great desert of white and then the common on the left with its First World War memorial water trough, its ice thick and hard as metal. I could have crossed the main road (just a Ford Consul gingerly making its way down the cleared centre) and walked up Green Lane past the dark cedars lining the entrance to a grand doorway just visible three quarter view. I could have passed the old people's flats, the nearly empty car park, the corner sweet shop/tobacconist closed and lightless, the coffee bar where I'd dawdled the day before, the outfitters, Cullens store and the new office scheme on the corner each scaffold pole bearing a topping of snow.

I could have crossed Murray Road passing Swannell and Sly the estate agents and then crossed the hump of the railway bridge to Station Road, on the right glimpsing on the far side the Post-Office Georgian bank and the bulk of the new shopping parade, Pages the builders and Bowleys the shoe shop. I could have turned down Station Road, down the steep pavement to the station entrance with its timber filigree canopy. I could have bought a return to Chalk Farm from the yawning ticket man with brylcreemed hair that he parted with surgical precision.

I could have paced up and down the empty platform for ten minutes then waited for five more behind the streaming window of the waiting room where a coated man would have been shuffling and re-shuffling the pages of his Sunday Express. I could have got up on hearing the train trundling in, its flat square face marked Baker Street and its wooden panelled carriages with heavy, leather-strapped windows. I could have entered a compartment through the heavy door with its distinctive slam – like the last word in an argument and I would have noticed the steamed up windows on which an elderly, scruffy man was amusing himself drawing cartoons with his finger.

I could have watched the familiar stations unroll, even then branded onto my unconscious geography of the world called Northwood and the places that could be reached from it: Northwood Hills — Pinner — North Harrow — Harrow-on-the-Hill — Northwick Park — Preston Road — Wembley Park and then the sprint past the inner suburb stations such as Neasden, Dollis Hill, Kilburn and West Hampstead to stop at Finchley Road where you could see rats on the line. And there a dark, intense man wearing a black leather jacket would have got in with a clatter of doors along the train behind him and he would have settled opposite the old man to stare gloomily out the window. I could have entered the tunnel, cave walls flickering with sparks and the pinned wires becoming an unending stream of whizzing parallels and then exited suddenly into open marshalling yards with high snow-crowned stock walls then back into the tunnel, to slow down then crawl in to Platform 1 at Baker Street. I could have walked over the trails of wet and mottled dirt, checked the Route map: Circle to Kings Cross/St Pancras then the Northern line to Chalk Farm.

I could have taken the steps down to the old Baker Street station and caught the first train in with its squeaks and rushing and gone through blackness to Great Portland street (glimpse of a girl in a beret), Euston Square then out at King's Cross. I could have followed signs through the labyrinth with its leering, repetitive gallery of ads for Players and with smiling Sunshine girls with chewing gum wads stuck on their mouths, to the strange Northern line, black on the route map. I could have found the north-bound platform, caught the first squat train and then, concentrating now, passed Mornington Crescent, Camden Town then, standing before I needed to, could have stepped out onto the platform at Chalk Farm.

And there passed the cream and purple Victorian tiles to the lift where two men in duffle coats would be talking in low voices; one laughing and the other moving his head sideways as if he had a tic. I could have taken the lift and walked out of the arches.

I would have been momentarily bewildered by the roar of traffic hissing through the black slush and the cold bite of air after the body warmth of the train. I could have looked at the street map. I could have crossed to Bridge Approach and seen a fox dart through the undergrowth behind the houses in Adelaide Road. I could have crossed the steel girders and rivets of the bridge as a train grumbled beneath then turned left past Primrose Hill station in to Gloucester Walk as hurrying and anonymous figures would have passed heading for the underground. I could have turned down Gloucester Road passing the Pembroke Castle with its stucco pillars and Victorian glass, passing the fleur-de-lis topped railings as the blare of Adelaide Road receded and an absorbed quietness replaced it. I could have noticed the lights on behind the big mock-Regency windows, (a man would be reading a newspaper, a woman drawing curtains) and then could have turned right into Fitzroy Road. I could have found the odd numbers, and crossed to the left and walked up to the crossroads, the Princess of Wales on the corner just about to open: a tall man in a donkey jacket would be waiting outside.

I could have crossed the road and noticed the car with the engine running and the coat-less woman and the two children going up the steps of the unlit house and her fiddling with the lock and the little girl mock-stamping her feet and the door finally opening and I would have run forward ...

And then what?

Could I simply have become an acne-speckled, awkward intrusion into this woman's evening? Could I have simply said I'd read her poems, that I'd heard her on the radio and found them very moving and did she have a copy she could let me have. I could have gestured and blarnied and tried to look vulnerable and harmless enough to be invited in. 'It's cold. You'd better come up – but not for long. Here carry this.' she might have said eventually, a trembling edge to her voice. And somehow the car would have gone and I would have entered the spotless, antiseptic flat and I could have ... well what?

I could have noticed the balloons, noticed, but not understood, the engraving of Isis, smelt the tang of apples, seen perhaps a desk strewn with papers and two sealed envelopes. I could have perched on a chair edge smiling at the little girl. But her mother would eventually, no quite soon, perhaps after a charitable mug of tea, simply have said, 'You must go' without a smile. And I would have gone, let there be no mistake, I would have gone. Of course.

But maybe the absurdity of it: the sudden arrival of this odd, middle-class youth with his gum-boots, school scarf and ridiculous rain-coat, his almost comic, gauche and breathless admiration would have been enough to prise just one iron bar from the cage, just enough. Just enough to stop her doing what she was going to do.

I could have.

Oversteps Books Ltd

The Oversteps list includes books by the following poets:

David Grubb, Giles Goodland, Alex Smith, Will Daunt, Patricia Bishop, Christopher Cook, Jan Farquarson, Charles Hadfield, Mandy Pannett, Doris Hulme, James Cole, Helen Kitson, Bill Headdon, Avril Bruton, Marianne Larsen, Anne Lewis-Smith, Mary Maher, Genista Lewes, Miriam Darlington, Anne Born, Glen Phillips, Rebecca Gethin, W H Petty, Melanie Penycate, Andrew Nightingale, Caroline Carver, John Stuart, Ann Segrave, Rose Cook, Jenny Hope, Christopher North, Hilary Elfick, Jennie Osborne, Anne Stewart, Oz Hardwick, Angela Stoner, Terry Gifford, Michael Swan, Denise Bennett, Maggie Butt, Anthony Watts, Joan McGavin, Robert Stein, Graham High, Ross Cogan, Ann Kelley, A C Clarke, Diane Tang, Susan Taylor, R V Bailey, Alwyn Marriage, John Daniel, Simon Williams, Kathleen Kummer, Jean Atkin, Charles Bennett, Elisabeth Rowe, Marie Marshall, Ken Head, Robert Cole, Cora Greenhill, John Torrance and Michael Bayley.

For details of all these books, information about Oversteps and up-to-date news, please look at our website:

www.overstepsbooks.com